are

are you ready?

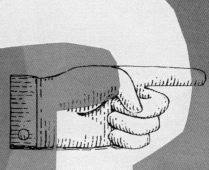

HOLLYWOOD

NEW

SUNSET BLVD

BUY

SALE

IMMACULATE
HEART
COLLEGE

PACIFIC
OCEAN

LOS ANGELES
C A L I F O R N I A

SIGNS OF HOPE

THE REVOLUTIONARY ART OF SISTER CORITA KENT

WORDS BY

MARA ROCKLIFF

PICTURES BY

MELISSA SWEET

ABRAMS BOOKS FOR YOUNG READERS

NEW YORK

The art for this book was made with collage and watercolor using hand-painted papers, printmaking, gouache, vintage magazines, pencil, and mixed media.

Cataloging-in-Publication Data has been applied for and may be obtained from the Library of Congress.

ISBN 978-1-4197-5221-6

Published in 2024 by Abrams Books for Young Readers, an imprint of ABRAMS.

Printed and bound in China
10 9 8 7 6 5 4 3 2 1

Abrams Books for Young Readers are available at special discounts when purchased in quantity for premiums and promotions as well as fundraising or educational use. Special editions can also be created to specification. For details, contact specialsales@abramsbooks.com or the address below.

Abrams® is a registered trademark of Harry N. Abrams, Inc.

ABRAMS The Art of Books
195 Broadway, New York, NY 10007
abramsbooks.com

FOR COURTNEY, HEATHER,
AND OF COURSE MELISSA—
THANK YOU FOR THIS
JOYFUL SIGN OF HOPE

—M.R.

TO ALL MY
MENTORS AND TEACHERS,
WITH GRATITUDE

—M.S.

Sister Corita teaches us to SEE
what everybody sees
but doesn't see.

Ordinary street signs,
ugly billboards,
posters no one pays attention to.

Sister Corita pays attention.
She sees nothing ordinary, nothing ugly.
She sees ART.

We look through a *finder*—
a small square of cardboard
with a hole cut out.

ALWAYS BE READY TO SEE WHAT YOU HAVEN'T SEEN BEFORE.

It helps us focus on the world a little at a time.

Our classroom is noisy, messy, and exciting.
She has us draw with our eyes closed, or
upside down, or with a chopstick dipped in ink.
Sometimes we have to make a hundred
drawings in one night. Another time,
we spend an hour staring at a bottle.
We forget if it is work or play.

Sister Corita
doesn't think
there is one
right way to
make art.

THE VERY WORD IMAGINATION IMPLIES tHAT YOU ARE INTO TERRITORY NO ONE HAS EVER BEEN TO be·fore.

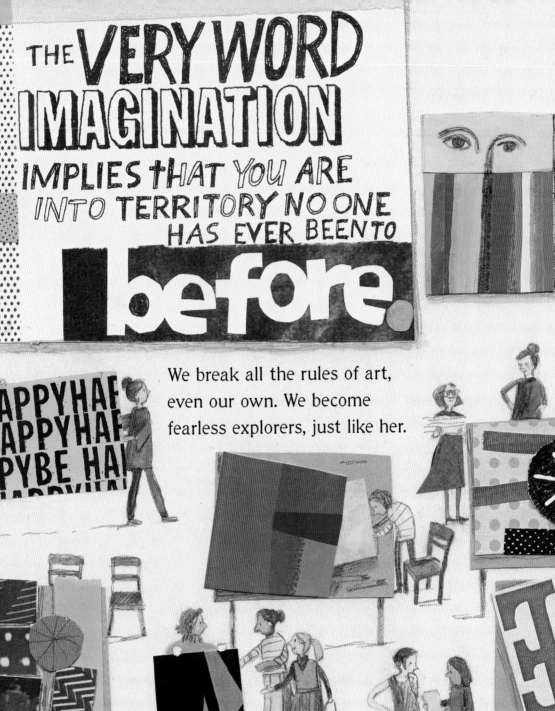

We break all the rules of art, even our own. We become fearless explorers, just like her.

She is always calm and always busy. Late at night, light spills under her door as she gathers her words.

Sister Corita shows us how to play with words. She liberates them from the pages of the glossy magazines called *LOOK* and *LIFE*. The big, shimmering letters curl and twist and crinkle in her hands. Even Sister Corita is surprised to see what the words really want to say.

We help her stretch the silk across a
wooden frame to make her stencil.
The word shapes wiggle, wave, and
wander off the frame.

The studio is small and bright. The air is hot and heavy with the smell of paint. Sister Corita pushes up the sleeves of her wool habit. Her strong arms drag thick paint across the screen—once, twice, a hundred times.

We hang up the wet prints, clean screens, mix the next batch of paint.

Happy Happy

SO much better

LEAP FOR JOY !

She is small and quiet, but
her art is big and loud.
As we walk past, it grabs us,
makes us STOP and LOOK.

Moving closer, we discover more words:
poetry, song lyrics, sentences that slipped
out of Sister Corita's magazines and books.
The tiny words invite us to read slowly.
They take time.

She takes us to galleries.
We see how other artists paint
everyday things like comic books
and cans of soup.

They call it Pop Art.
Art collectors pay high prices for
works by these famous men.

Sister Corita sells her prints from the back of a van.
She is happy to make art that anyone can own.

Together, we plan a special day. We celebrate with giant banners, barefoot dancing, extra colors, extra sounds.

But not everything is beautiful.
In the news and on the streets, we see
injustice, inequality, prejudice, poverty.
Sister Corita's words go on the march.

this
war
MUST
stop

END POVERTY

END
THE WAR
IN VIETNAM

2200+
WAR DEAD

A time
of dreams
unfulfilled

NOW!

peace

THE PERSON WHO MAKES THINGS IS A SIGN OF HOPE

SHOULD LIKE TO BE ABLE TO LOVE MY COUNTRY AND STILL LOVE JUSTICE.

-Camus

There is anger in her art, but also joy. "The joyous revolutionary," she is called.

LOOK

50 CENTS · DECEMBER 30, 1969

Now people STOP and LOOK and pay attention to this revolutionary nun.

EDUCATOR, ARTIST, GENTLE REVOLUTIONARY

WONDER

LET THE MORNING TIME DROP ALL ITS PETALS ON ME. LIFE, I LOVE YOU.

THE NUN:
GONE MODERN

Men with cameras crowd into
our classroom, eager to claim Sister Corita
for a movie or a glossy magazine.

The art that anyone can own
is mounted on museum walls.
Companies sell a copy of her style.

Late at night, light spills under her
door again. She struggles to find sleep.

Sister Corita goes away.
Beside the ocean, she can focus
on the world a little at a time.

She turns over the words in her heart
to find out what they want to say.

THE GROUND WORK DOESN'T SHOW UNTIL ONE DAY.

She has taught us how to SEE
and play
and protest joyfully,
to make art all our lives
and to make our lives ART.
Now it's our turn to share what we have learned.

SHE TAUGHT THAT ART IS NOT SOMETHING APART FROM LIFE AND LIVING.

EVERYTHING WAS A JOY TO HER... AND THAT'S CATCHING.

IMAGINATION IS EVERYTHING

I DIDN'T KNOW THAT I COULD SEE THE WAY THAT AN ARTIST SEES.

SHE DIDN'T TEACH US HOW TO DRAW OR PAINT SO MUCH AS **SHE TAUGHT US** TO **CARE.**

THERE AREN'T MANY LESSONS MORE VALUABLE THAN TO PAY ATTENTION.

WHEN YOU HAVE A GREAT TEACHER, THAT PERSON LIVES WITH **YOU** THROUGHOUT YOUR **LIFE.** YOU HAVE PUT A LITTLE BIT OF THEM INTO YOURSELF.

AUTHOR'S noTe

Sister Corita Kent was born Frances Elizabeth Kent in Fort Dodge, Iowa, on November 20, 1918. She was the fifth of six children. When she was little, her family moved to Vancouver, British Columbia, and then to Hollywood, California. The children went to Catholic school, where they were taught by nuns.

Frances loved to play with crayons, paper, and scissors. She drew posters and made paper dolls. Seeing her talent, her sixth-grade teacher gave her private art lessons after school.

At the age of eighteen, Frances decided to become a nun. She joined the Order of the Immaculate Heart of Mary and took Sister Mary Corita as her religious name.

After graduating from Immaculate Heart College, an all-women's college run by the IHM sisters, she was sent to teach school in Canada. Three years later, Sister Corita was called back to Los Angeles to join the art department at IHC, where she soon became a popular teacher.

Sister Corita also studied for a master's degree in art history at the University of Southern California. Too busy to take the long bus ride to the USC campus for a printmaking workshop, she taught herself how to make silkscreen prints.

After seeing Andy Warhol's *Campbell's Soup Cans* at the Ferus Gallery in 1962, she began using advertising slogans in her art along with other familiar words and images, combining them in unexpected ways. Instead of selling Wonder Bread or Pepsi-Cola, Sister Corita's eye-catching posters sold ideas like peace, hope, gratitude, justice, equality, and love.

By the late 1960s, America was in turmoil, with protests against racism and the ongoing war in Vietnam. Father Daniel Berrigan, a Jesuit priest and close friend of Sister Corita, was one of the "Catonsville Nine," a group of Catholic activists arrested for an act of civil disobedience against what many considered an immoral war. Sister Corita admired the courage of the Catonsville Nine and tried to emulate it in her art with prints that juxtaposed words and images in unexpected ways to make viewers think more deeply about world events.

As her art became well-known, Sister Corita's life got busier and busier. In addition to teaching day, evening, and weekend classes and running the art department, along with daily prayers and chores, she traveled, exhibited, lectured, and gave interviews. She was able to make prints for only three weeks every year.

Her difficulties were increased by a conflict within the church. Inspired by the push for modernization of the Second Vatican Council (1962-1965) and the changes happening around them, the IHM sisters began making changes in their own religious life, such as choosing to give up their traditional habits and instead wear ordinary street clothes like the people they served. The archbishop of Los Angeles, already a harsh critic of Sister Corita's art, banned the sisters from teaching in Catholic schools.

In 1968, on a trip to Cape Cod, Massachusetts, Sister Corita realized she couldn't do it anymore. After more than thirty years in the Order of the Immaculate Heart of Mary, she decided not to return.

Corita Kent went on making art, including the "Rainbow Swash" she painted on a giant gas tank—now a Boston landmark—as well as her 1985 LOVE postage stamp, of which more than 700 million were sold. She died in 1986. Former students—and their students, and *their* students—still talk about how, thanks to Corita, they learned to keep two things open: their eyes, and their minds.

TIMELINE

1918 Born Frances Elizabeth Kent on November 20 in Fort Dodge, Iowa

1923 Family moves to Los Angeles, California

1936 Enters Order of the Immaculate Heart of Mary, becomes Sister Mary Corita

1947 Begins teaching art at Immaculate Heart College

1951 Learns screen printing

1962 Andy Warhol's *Campbell's Soup Cans* exhibit inspires Corita to make Pop Art prints

1965 United States enters the Vietnam War

Campbell's CHICKEN NOODLE SOUP

bloom

DREAM

MIND-BLOWING YEAR

electronic art beat

1966	*Los Angeles Times* names Corita one of nine Women of the Year	**1971**	Boston Gas Company asks Corita to create a design for one of its 140-foot-tall gas tanks, which becomes the largest copyrighted artwork in the world
1967	Corita appears on the cover of *Newsweek*		
	Supreme Court case *Loving v. Virginia* overturns laws against interracial marriage[*]	**1974**	Corita is diagnosed with cancer
1968	Catonsville Nine activists, led by Corita's friend Daniel Berrigan, arrested for burning draft records in protest of the Vietnam War[*]	**1983**	Corita designs billboards saying WE CAN CREATE LIFE WITHOUT WAR, calling them the most religious work she's ever done
	Martin Luther King Jr. assassinated[*]	**1985**	United States Postal Service issues Corita's LOVE stamp
	After taking time away in Cape Cod, Massachusetts, Corita decides to leave the Order of the Immaculate Heart of Mary	**1986**	Corita dies September 18 in Boston, Massachusetts

[*]See Corita's works *new hope* (1966), *if i* (1969), *king's dream* (1969), and *phil and dan* (1969), among others.

iLLUSTRATOR'S NOTE

My first introduction to Corita Kent was seeing her signature swashes on the Boston Gas Company's tanks along the highway. The freedom of those bold and dashing marks had a timeless quality and inspired me as a young artist. Working on this book all these years later, Corita's ways of creating reminded me of my wonderful teachers and mentors and all the other people who encouraged me in my lifetime of making art.

Quotes from Corita, hand-lettered as part of this book's art, include a few of the famous "rules" for making art that she wrote with her students. My favorite is Rule 4: *Consider everything an experiment.* It gives us permission to play and leads to new ideas, serendipity, and creativity. Most important is Corita's tenet that life and art are inseparable. That's my experience, too.

MAKE YOUR OWN FINDER!

It's easy to make your own finder. Just cut a square hole in a small piece of cardboard. (Ask for help if you need it.)

Look through the hole, close-up, at little pieces of the world. Be ready to see things that you have never seen before!

A phone camera works as a finder, too. Or use your fingers to frame what you see.

SOURCES FOR QUOTES

Page 9   "One purpose of art . . .": Corita Kent quoted in Corita Kent and Jan Steward, *Learning by Heart: Teachings to Free the Creative Spirit*, 2nd ed. New York: Allworth Press, 2008 (p. 32).

Page 11   "Always be ready . . .": Corita Kent quoted in *Learning by Heart* (p. 30).

Page 13   "The very word *imagination* . . .": Corita Kent quoted in *Learning by Heart* (p. 60).

Page 14   "It is necessary to turn the words over . . .": Corita Kent quoted in Jennifer L. Roberts, "Backwords: Screen Printing and the Politics of Reversal," from Susan Dackerman (ed.), *Corita Kent and the Language of Pop.* Cambridge, MA: Harvard Art Museums, 2015 (p. 61). Cites original source as "Pop-Artist Nun Finds Salvation in Beatles," *Yale Daily News*, March 14, 1966.

Page 19   "Be happy whenever you can manage it . . .": "Immaculate Heart College Art Department Rules," developed by Corita Kent and the Immaculate Heart College Art Department, Rule 9. From April Dammann, *Corita Kent: Art and Soul—The Biography*. Santa Monica, CA: Angel City Press, 2015 (p. 77).

Page 20   "The commonplace is not worthless . . .": Corita Kent quoted in *Learning by Heart* (p. 13).

Page 23   "There is no line . . .": Corita Kent quoted in *Learning by Heart* (p. 35).

Page 25   "The person who makes things . . .": Corita Kent quoted in "The Nun: A Joyous Revolution," *Newsweek*, December 25, 1967. "And I should like to be able to love . . .": Quote by Albert Camus, referenced in Corita's piece *e eye love*, included in Ian Berry and Michael Duncan (ed.), *Someday Is Now: The Art of Corita Kent*. New York: Frances Young Tang Teaching Museum and Art Gallery at Skidmore College and DelMonico Books, 2013 (p. 183).

Page 26   "Let the morning time drop . . .": lyric by Paul Simon, referenced in Corita's piece *life is a complicated business* included in Ian Berry and Michael Duncan (ed.), *Someday Is Now: The Art of Corita Kent* (p. 147).

Page 27   "Nothing is a mistake . . .": "Immaculate Heart College Art Department Rules," Rule 6. "How would you describe yourself?": Corita Kent quoted in, *Corita Kent: Art and Soul—The Biography* (p. 149; attributed to 1984 interview).

Page 29   "The ground work doesn't show . . .": slightly paraphrased from Corita's piece *one day*, included in *Someday Is Now: The Art of Corita Kent* (p. 215).

Page 30   "She taught that art . . .": former student Jan Steward in *Learning by Heart* (p. 6). "Everything was a joy to her . . .": former student Marie Egan (3:48) in *Become a Microscope* by Aaron Rose (director); see www.youtube.com/watch?v=EaOWOULeH-0.

Page 31   "I didn't know that I could see . . .": former student Barbara Turner (7:08), "There aren't many lessons . . .": former student Helen Kelley (21:30), "When you have a great teacher . . .": filmmaker Baylis Glascock (21:09), all from *Become a Microscope*. "She didn't teach us . . .": former student quoted in *Learning by Heart* (p. 35).

WHERE TO LEARN MORE ABOUT CORITA KENT

Corita.org is the website of the Corita Art Center, a project of the Immaculate Heart Community. This website offers lots of information about Corita's life and work, along with a close-up look at many of her colorful prints.

BOOKS WITH PICTURES OF CORITA'S ART

Ault, Julie. *Come Alive! The Spirited Art of Sister Corita.* London: Four Corners Books, 2006.

Dackerman, Susan, ed. *Corita Kent and the Language of Pop.* Cambridge, MA: Harvard Art Museums, 2015.

Dammann, April. *Corita Kent: Art and Soul—The Biography.* Santa Monica, CA: Angel City Press, 2015.

CORITA IN HER OWN WORDS

Galm, Bernard. "Interview of Corita Kent" (transcript). UCLA Library Center for Oral History Research, April 6, 13, and 20, 1976. See oralhistory.library.ucla.edu.

Glascock, Baylis. "We have no art" (video footage). Catherine G. Murphy Gallery, 1967. See www.youtube.com/watch?v=-VjtvgCGrWg.

Kent, Corita, and Jan Steward. *Learning by Heart,* 2nd ed. New York: Allworth Press, 2008. (Originally published 1992, six years after Corita's death.)

WHAT PEOPLE SAID ABOUT CORITA AT THE TIME

Adler, Nancy. "Nun's Art Class Has Modern View." *New York Times,* July 17, 1967.

"The Nun: A Joyous Revolution." *Newsweek,* December 25, 1967.

WHAT PEOPLE HAVE SAID MORE RECENTLY

Moorhead, Joanna. "Corita Kent, the Pop Art Nun." *Guardian,* April 22, 2018.

Rose, Aaron, director. *Become a Microscope: 90 Statements on Sister Corita* (2014). See www.nowness.com/series/directors-cuts/dc-aaron-rose.

"Sister Mary Corita Kent's LA Studio Designated Historical Landmark." *Artforum,* June 3, 2021.